D1609436

Meyersdale Public Library
210 Cent
P.O. B
Meyersdale, PA

WITHDRAWN

796.3
Temple

AR
4.8

37955

SHAQUILLE
O'NEAL

SHAQUILLE
O'NEAL

BOB TEMPLE
THE CHILD'S WORLD®, INC.

ON THE COVER...

Front cover: Shaquille concentrates on the ball during a 1998 game against the Los Angeles Clippers.
Page 2: Shaquille takes a break from a 1997 game against the Detroit Pistons.

Published in the United States of America by The Child's World®, Inc.
PO Box 326
Chanhassen, MN 55317-0326
800-599-READ
www.childsworld.com

Product Manager Mary Berendes
Editor Katherine Stevenson
Designer Mary Berendes

Photo Credits
© AFP/CORBIS: 9
© AP/WideWorld Photos: 16, 19
© Brian Drake/SportsChrome-USA: 15
© David L. Johnson/SportsChrome-USA: 10, 13
© Michael Zito/SportsChrome-USA: 2
© Reuters NewMedia Inc./CORBIS: 6, 20, 22
© SportsChrome-USA: cover

Copyright © 2001 by The Child's World®, Inc.
All rights reserved. No part of this book may be
reproduced or utilized in any form or by any means
without written permission from the publisher.

Library of Congress Cataloging-in-Publication Data
Temple, Bob.
Shaquille O'Neal / by Bob Temple.
p. cm.
Includes index.
ISBN 1-56766-969-7
1. O'Neal, Shaquille—Juvenile literature.
2. Basketball players—United States—Biography—Juvenile literature.
[1. O'Neal, Shaquille. 2. Basketball players. 3. Afro-Americans—Biography.]
I. Title.
GV884.O46 T46 2001
796.323'092—dc21

00-011884

TABLE OF CONTENTS

A CHAMPION

Shaquille O'Neal stood on the basketball **court** at the Staples Center in Los Angeles. His teammates were screaming and yelling, bouncing all over, and hugging each other. Shaquille's family was all around him. At 7-foot-1 and 330 pounds, Shaquille is a powerful figure. But this time, Shaquille was crying.

Shaquille and his team, the Los Angeles Lakers, had just won the 2000 NBA **championship.** It was the first championship of Shaquille's career, and his tears were tears of joy. It made him especially happy because a lot of people thought he might never win a championship.

But Shaquille proved them all wrong. Not only did the Lakers win the championship, but Shaquille was also voted the Most Valuable Player of the playoffs.

"I've waited eight years of my life for this to happen, and it finally happened," Shaquille said.

Shaquille is presented with the Most Valuable Player trophy after the Lakers won the 2000 NBA Finals against the Indiana Pacers.

LITTLE BIG MAN

Shaquille was born on March 6, 1972. His mother, Lucille, named him "Shaquille" because it means "Little Warrior" in Arabic. They lived in Newark, New Jersey. Early in his life, Shaquille did not have a father in his house. In the early 1970s, Lucille married Philip Harrison, who became Shaquille's father. Because Philip was in the army, the family moved to a different city every three years. They even lived in West Germany for a while.

Every time the family moved, Shaquille had to make new friends. That was hard for him. By the time he was 13 years old, Shaquille was 6-foot-5, taller than most grown men. Other kids made fun of his height and his unusual name. "My parents told me to be proud," he said. "But I wasn't. I wanted to be normal." Over time, Shaquille learned that it was okay to stand out above the crowd.

Because he found it difficult to fit in, Shaquille wasn't happy. He got into trouble as a child. He acted out in school. Shaquille's father was in the army and was very strict. He wanted his son to grow up to be a respectable man.

Shaquille works against Mark Jackson of the Indiana Pacers during game 4 of the 2000 NBA Finals.

→

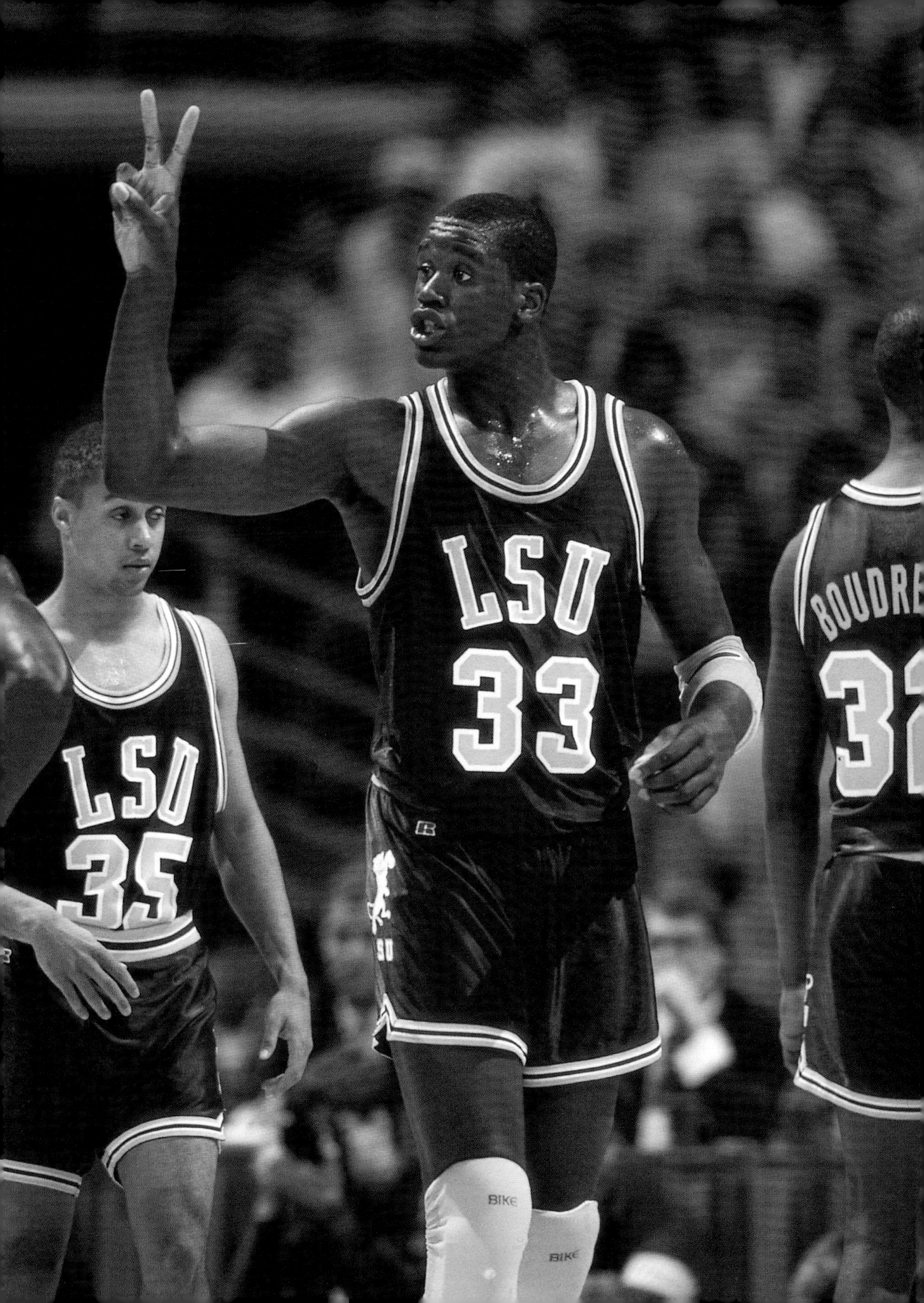
LSU
33
LSU
35
BOUDRE
32
BIKE
BIKE

FINDING AN OUTLET

Shaquille needed an activity to help him stay out of trouble. Basketball was the answer. On the basketball court, Shaquille's size helped him. The other kids wanted to be on his team, which made him feel better. And the more he played basketball, the better he became.

When he was 13 and living in West Germany, he met Dale Brown, the basketball coach at Louisiana State University. Because Shaquille was so big, the coach asked him how long he had been in the army. "I'm only 13," Shaquille said. Coach Brown asked Shaquille to think about playing at LSU when he was old enough.

HIGH SCHOOL STAR

In February of 1987, Philip Harrison and the family moved again, this time to Fort Sam Houston in San Antonio, Texas. There Shaquille joined the basketball team at Cole High School. The Cole Cougars were tough to beat with Shaquille on the team. In his junior year, Shaquille averaged 18 points and more than 13 **rebounds** per game. Before his senior year began, he had grown to 6-foot-11, and every major college team in the country wanted him. His summer team in San Antonio had won the national championship. He decided to go to LSU and play for Coach Brown, the man he had met in West Germany.

Shaquille signals to an LSU teammate during a 1990 game.

Before his senior season started, Shaquille spent a lot of time in the weight room. He lifted weights to add muscle to his tall frame. By the time the season started, he weighed 240 pounds. No one could stop him. He averaged almost 30 points and over 21 rebounds per game, and Cole won the Class 3A Texas state championship. During Shaquille's two seasons at Cole, the Cougars won 68 games and lost only one.

ON TO LSU

In the fall of 1989, Shaquille enrolled at LSU. By then, he was a nationally known basketball star who was joining an already successful team. Two other players, Stanley Roberts and Chris Jackson, had made LSU one of the best teams in the country. With Shaquille now playing with them, they were ranked No. 2 in the country by the Associated Press.

Having Roberts and Jackson as teammates helped Shaquille, because he didn't have to carry his team alone. He was able to get used to playing college basketball without having to be his team's main scorer. It also helped that Shaquille grew two more inches, to 7-foot-1, and bulked up to 290 pounds!

In Shaquille's freshman season, the LSU Tigers were good, but not as good as many people expected. Shaquille averaged almost 14 points and 12 rebounds per game, but the Tigers lost in the second round of the NCAA Tournament.

An exhausted Shaquille takes a break during a 1990 LSU game.

After that loss, Jackson and Roberts both announced that they were going to turn **professional** and play in the NBA. That left Shaquille as the lone star on the LSU team.

In his second year, Shaquille jumped into the spotlight and enjoyed being the star. It was a difficult season for him, though. Since he was the only star on the team, the Tigers' opponents often used three players to guard him. He was always getting banged, bumped, and bruised. Still, he averaged 27.6 points and 14.7 rebounds per game and was named college basketball player of the year. Shaquille hurt his left leg before the NCAA Tournament, however, and the Tigers lost in the first round.

TURNING PRO

Shaquille stayed in college for one more year. He averaged 24.1 points and 14 rebounds, but once more the Tigers lost in the second round of the NCAA Tournament. Shaquille had grown frustrated by the way other teams guarded him. Even though Shaquille could have stayed in college for one more season, Coach Brown told him he should go to the NBA. NBA rules would make it harder for teams to use two or three players to guard him. On April 3, 1992, Shaquille announced that he was leaving LSU to become a professional basketball player.

Shaquille wears an Orlando Magic hat as he answers questions at a press conference after the 1992 draft.

THE MAGIC KINGDOM

In the summer of 1992, the Orlando Magic selected Shaquille with the first overall pick in the NBA **draft.** It didn't take Shaquille long to make a name for himself, both on the court and off. Before he even signed his first pro **contract,** he signed a deal for his own line of basketball shoes. He also starred in television commercials. On the court, he was a powerful player from the start. He was named the league's Player of the Week in the first week of the season, and Player of the Month in the first month of the season. No **rookie** had ever done that before.

But Shaquille also had his critics. Some people thought that all he could do was dunk the ball. They didn't think he was a good shooter. But Shaquille was also good at blocking shots and rebounding. He finished his rookie season ranked second in the league in blocked shots, averaging 3.53 per game. He was also second in rebounding, averaging 13.9, and eighth in scoring, at 23.4 points per game. More importantly, he had made the Magic a better team. The year before Shaquille arrived, the Magic had won only 21 of 82 games. In Shaquille's first year, the Magic went 41–41. That was 20 more wins than the year before! He was named the NBA's Rookie of the Year.

Shaquille dunks the ball over Sacramento Kings forward Michael Smith during a 1994 game.

MOVING UP

In his second year, the Magic added Anfernee "Penny" Hardaway to their team and became one of the best teams in the NBA. Shaquille's game kept getting better and better, too. Every year he added new skills, such as a little hook shot. He began to gain more respect. But one thing always held him back. Shaquille was not a very good free-throw shooter. Even today, Shaquille has trouble with that part of his game. Most NBA players make about 75 percent of their free throws, but Shaquille makes only about 50 percent.

Still, he and his team were successful. In the 1994–95 season, Shaquille led the league in scoring. The Magic made it all the way to the NBA Finals before losing to the Houston Rockets. Shaquille had come close to his dream of winning the NBA Championship but had fallen just short.

GOING TO LOS ANGELES

In 1996, Shaquille had a busy year. He was named one of the 50 greatest players in NBA history, even though he had played for only four years. In the summer, he played in the Olympics on the U.S. men's basketball team, helping the team win the gold medal. And he was traded to the Los Angeles Lakers. Shaquille continued to dominate the league, but the Lakers couldn't win a championship.

Shaquille works hard during a game against Argentina in the 1996 Olympics.

A NEW COACH

Finally, going into the 1999–2000 season, the Lakers seemed ready to win a championship. Shaquille was better than ever. Phil Jackson, who had coached Michael Jordan and the Chicago Bulls to six championships, was now the Lakers' coach.

Shaquille had his best season ever. He led the league in scoring, averaging 29.7 points, and was second in rebounds, at 13.6 per game. In one game on March 6, he scored 61 points against the Los Angeles Clippers. For the first time, Shaquille was named the league's Most Valuable Player.

In the playoffs, he was even better. In the NBA Finals against the Indiana Pacers, he averaged 38.0 points and 16.7 rebounds per game. The Lakers won the series, four games to two.

A CHAMPION AT LAST

When the buzzer sounded and the Lakers were champions, Shaquille celebrated and cried. He had finally achieved what he had worked so hard to do. "I've held my emotions for about 11 years now," Shaquille said. "Three years of college, eight years in the league, always wanting to win. It just came out."

But those tears were tears of happiness. "I worked very hard to get here, and it was an emotional game," he said. "I'm happy for my teammates. I'm happy for the city. It's just a great moment!"

Shaquille kisses the Most Valuable Player trophy
after the Lakers won the 2000 NBA Finals.

TIMELINE

March 6, 1972	Shaquille O'Neal is born in Newark, New Jersey.
1985	At age 13, Shaquille meets LSU coach Dale Brown in West Germany.
1987	Shaquille enrolls at Cole High School in San Antonio, Texas.
1988	Shaquille's summer team wins the national championship.
1989	Shaquille averages 30 points per game and leads Cole High School to the state championship.
Fall 1989	Shaquille enrolls at LSU.
1990	LSU loses in the second round of the NCAA tournament.
1991	Shaquille is named college basketball's Player of the Year.
1992	Shaquille announces he is leaving LSU for the NBA Draft and is drafted first overall by the Orlando Magic.
1993	Shaquille is named NBA Rookie of the Year.
1995	Shaquille leads the Magic to the NBA Finals.
1996	Shaquille is named one of the 50 greatest players in NBA history. He also helps the U. S. men's Olympic basketball team win the gold medal and is traded to the Los Angeles Lakers.
2000	Shaquille is named the NBA's Most Valuable Player, leads the Lakers to the NBA championship, and is named MVP of the NBA Finals.

Shaquille smiles and jokes with reporters during a 2000 press conference.

GLOSSARY

championship (CHAM-pee-un-ship)
A championship is a game or series of games that decides the best person or team in a sport. Shaquille O'Neal and the Los Angeles Lakers won the NBA championship in 2000.

contract (KON-trakt)
A contract is the agreement an athlete signs when he or she is hired by a team. Shaquille O'Neal signed a contract to play for the Orlando Magic in 1992.

court (KORT)
In basketball, the court is the floor and baskets where the game is played. After he won the NBA championship, Shaquille O'Neal cried on the court because he was so happy.

draft (DRAFT)
In professional sports, the draft is the way in which teams choose new players. Shaquille O'Neal was the first player picked in the 1992 NBA Draft.

professional (pro-FESH-un-ull)
In sports, a professional is someone good enough to get paid instead of just playing for fun. Shaquille O'Neal is a professional basketball player.

rebounds (REE-bowndz)
In basketball, getting a rebound is gaining control of the ball after someone misses a basket. Shaquille O'Neal is one of the best rebounders in the NBA.

rookie (ROOK-ee)
In professional sports, a player in his or her first year is called a rookie. Shaquille O'Neal was named NBA Rookie of the Year in 1993.

INDEX